Your child
the
Little Scientist

I0421948

Denisia Hockley

It Is What It Is!

This little book is not trying to be a full on hard cover parenting book! Rudolf Dreikurs already did that in the early eighties with *Happy Children*. He got it right then, and his words are still gold today. This hard-hitting, punchy little book is designed to get seriously important messages across to not just people who are currently parents or children but everyone. Everything you do, everything you are, stems from your hard drive, the programs written on your psychological, intellectual, and emotional computer since the day you were born (probably before). You are still a child inside, we all are, and that is a good thing! When all evidence of the childlike innocence, curiosity, and genius has gone, what do you have left?

Denisia J. Hockley

Dreikurs got the strategies and processes down pat; they are accurate, and they work. *The Little Scientist* is a quick read from which you will get insights and realizations that should be life changing, especially if you do have a young child and you apply this newfound wisdom to the things you are currently programming onto their hard drive. In this case, you will need to put your ego and guilt-indulgence to the side; do not get hung up on the mistakes you have made (if they were not mistakes, we would call them deliberates). Focus on change, growth, and developing nurturing relationships with

You
Your kids
Your Family

And

Everyone who has ever been a child!

CONTENTS

Introduction

To those mothers I have worked with over the years, I can't disclose names but you know who you are, especially my young mums from the Pinniger clinic who either had great parenting skills or used what I taught them to create wonderful little humans with a strong healthy sense of self.

Written for parents but aimed at children of all ages: people in schools, in colleges, and in maternity hospitals. Adults read it from the perspective of you as a child; parents read it to see your child as a person!

While the many years I have spent working with adult victims of child abuse has a significant impact on the reason for this book, the primary value is to teach you how the young mind and heart develops and how a person's core beliefs, attitudes, and emotional knowing is programmed from birth and reinforced both negatively and positively over time. We arrived on this planet with many innate concepts, some of which work against us, particularly in adolescence and later life. Ideally, in that first five to seven years, we have wise and involved parents who have the time and the knowledge to teach us not to reinforce guilt, self-doubt, and self-blame. I say "ideally" because rarely do even the most loving and caring parents have knowledge of these things let alone the time or skills to change them.

This is not about blame; parents, good and bad, essentially do the best they know how; based on their own history, attitudes, and core beliefs, but there is even more to this. When we look at how the little child's *emotional knowing* develops, we gain insight as to why parents *need* to repeat many of the mistakes their own parents made. This will unfold as you read on. You will notice I repeat some concepts that I have already covered; that is because you really need to *get* some of these messages so do bear repeating.

Something as important and complex as raising children and growing any relationship really can be put as simple as

focusing on what you want more of

and

ignoring what you do not want repeated !

My Kid? A Scientist? Really ?

When a behavior produces desired outcomes, it will be repeated; when a behavior produces unwanted outcomes, it may also be repeated a few times because as scientists we may need to repeat an experiment a few times in order to work out cause and effect, consistency of outcomes, variable correlations, and random effects. Yes, these technical *research* terms do apply to your child (and you now; and when you were a child and an adolescent and your parents, partners, boss, etcetera, etcetera).

Often mum works happily away at what she is doing, believing that because the children are playing nicely, she need not give them attention, but as soon as they start to squabble or fight among themselves, she will drop what she is doing and go over to them, which is giving focus to behavior she does not want repeated as well as teaching them inappropriate ways of getting her attention. Ideally, before they resort to the unwanted behavior, she would take a moment to go over and praise them for playing so well, but when they start to fight (unless someone is going to get seriously damaged) leave them alone and let them work it out for themselves. If it does get out of hand, calmly and quietly separate them without too much attention and certainly without taking sides; trust me, the little *victim* in the scenario is just as much a player in the "let's see who can get mum on who's side" game as the one doing the hitting or whatever. They are working together to get you involved; testing their territory to see who has the most control over mum and, of course, being little scientists, experiment with the cause and effect relationships between different behaviors and environmental outcomes.

We all started by being born into a world full of mysterious events; babies and children are egocentric, which means that they know full well that everything that happens in their universe happens as a consequence of them being in it. Yes, we can *know* things that are incorrect! So we (as children) see something cool happening over there and don't know how we did it, but we are pretty impressed with ourselves. Dad gets sick or angry, and we don't understand how we *caused* that. Here starts the path of a lifelong endeavor of trying to undo our mistakes, which is extremely difficult since we do not know what we did to cause it (mainly because we did not cause it). We may spend the rest of our lives trying to make up for not being good enough to stop our parents from fighting or mum from dying or little sister from being sick. Of course if the parents actually knew this was going on in the child's *knowing*, they would go to great lengths to correct this faulty thinking pattern being programmed onto junior's hard drive; we would go to great lengths to explain, teach, and reassure the child that they are not to blame for these events. Ideally, by the age of five or six, the child grasps that most things are not her/his fault; even so called "bad" behavior is more often than not an accident, mistake, or bad judgment call made by a tiny scientist who is trying to work out how the world works and how they can best make it work for them.

Children, do not do bad behaviors!

Okay, that statement just lost a few hard-core parents, but read on! Your child is a little scientist, working out cause and effect and logical consequences, which incidentally parents have a bad habit of screwing up by making the consequences of the child's actions far from logical. If missy goes to school without her lunch box, the logical consequence is she will get a little hungry that day. It is highly unlikely she will drop dead from

5

Denisia J. Hockley

starvation. Of course, mum cannot stand the idea of junior not having lunch, so she gets in the car and delivers the lunch to school. Okay, I am just as guilty as you. I did it. We all do it, and this example is not a huge one, but one we can all relate to because missy probably would not forget things so often if she just had to suffer the logical consequence when it happened the first couple of times. Remember now that logical consequence is *not punishment!* Punishment does *not* teach!

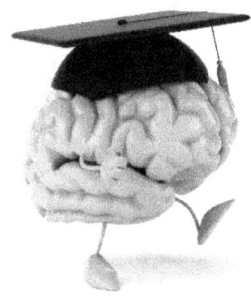

Childhood, parenting, life—it's all about learning. You also need to remember that from birth to adolescence, the boundaries and rules change regularly. The younger the child, the more confusing the changes, so they really do need to keep checking as to what is acceptable behavior *this week*.

"Yesterday, I was not allowed to feed myself, but today, you have given me my own spoon...interesting!"

"Last week, I was peeing in a diaper, but now I have big boy pants."

"Last week, you got really mad when I drew you a picture on the wall with vegemite, not sure if you didn't like my picture or the color, so I think I will make you a nice red one with jam. Painting with food is cool because I can lick my fingers after, and that's yummy."

"Okay, now you're yelling at me, something about I should know better because you told me last week. You're making me stand in the naughty corner, and I am very confused. I guess you still do not like my pictures. I wonder if I should stop using the spoon and maybe give you back the big boy pants. It is so hard to keep on top of these changes all the time. I will just have to keep experimenting until I get it right."

"I hate it when mum and dad fight because I never know what I did to cause it, and sometimes they tell me it's because I am too much trouble, and I don't even know why, guess I am probably just a bad kid. Maybe I will just give up on everything since I'm going to mess it up anyway, or maybe I will just keep trying to be more and more perfect and just accept that no matter how well I think I have done something, it will still always need doing better."

Are you starting to recognize the beginnings of certain adult traits that lead to perfectionism, obsessive needs to achieve, and fruitless striving for approval that never comes, or going the other way and giving up or not even trying because, let's face it, nothing will ever be good enough. You are, after all, a rather useless, hopeless failure. The less you attempt, the less you will screw up! It is just the way you have always been; you're wired that way.

No not wired! Programmed from a very early age!

From an early age, we learn to try different behaviors to fix our world. Fortunately, in a psychologically healthy environment by the time we are around five years old, we have learned that everything in fact was not our fault; mum told missy over and over that it was not her fault daddy left. Dad told junior repeatedly that he approved of him no matter what choices he made. Children need to learn from an early age that they do not need to jump through hoops to be *good enough* and they don't have to excel at dad's favorite sport in order to feel loved or get him to spend time with him.

It's relatively easy to recognize bad parenting behaviors, but what about parents that do everything by the book and still screw up? Mum and Dad give the kids heaps of attention, mountains of encouragement and opportunities to achieve great things. Yet missy drops out of school and gives up while junior becomes a stressed out overachiever. How do you win! You did everything right. Hmm. Unfortunately, there was so much emphasis placed on achievement that missy felt her efforts were never ever going to be quite good enough because every time she nearly reached the bar you raised it because you knew she could do better, and of course you only want the best for your child. That would have been okay if you had let her reach the goal, have her achievement acknowledged and positively reinforced for a while, and then maybe look at going to the next level. Or how about allowing it to be okay to be average or to just do something because it is fun and not necessarily be that good at it. As it is, she gave up because she learned that she was never actually going to be good enough.

Junior on the other hand worked out that if he pushed himself hard enough, he could almost keep up with the impossibly high standards required to make his parents happy. Sadly, his identity becomes dependent on success. While he is wearing his professional or academic or athletic *hat*, he is confident and self-assured, but if he takes off his *hats* and is left alone with his own *self*, he becomes anxious and insecure. Throughout life, we wear many hats: mother, boss, husband and such, but often midlife crisis comes about because retirement, loss of career, empty nest and the likes, leave you without a *hat*, without an identity. For the first time in your life, you have to settle for being just Jane, and that is frightening because she is no one in particular and has no credibility. In fact, without your identity hats, you crumble into an insecure ghost with no direction and no sense of self.

9

Take the example of a new mum with an eighteen-month-old toddler; he walks and falls and bumps into things because this walking thing is new, and he needs practice. Mum affectionately teases him for being clumsy. She doesn't even notice how many times a day she feeds the idea of being clumsy into his hard drive. He develops a *core belief*, an identity even, that he is clumsy. Of course, when he is eight or nine years old, he knows how to walk, but he also knows he is clumsy because true to his belief, he has continued to bump into and fall over things. There is nothing wrong with his motor coordination; physically he is fine. How can this be?

Every minute of your life your senses take in around two million pieces of information. Of course, you do not consciously process all of it; your brain might explode if you did. Your reticular activating system (RAS, which incidentally does many really cool things, this is only one of them) filters all this information and uses some of it to provide you with confirming evidence for your beliefs. So with all that stimuli to work with it is not hard to provide junior with opportunity to reinforce his clumsiness or any other *faulty* belief about himself, others, or the world. We have all known of someone who believes all men are abusive or all women cheat; they had an experience and developed a belief, and their RAS provided all the evidence they needed to keep believing this. It's a bit like statistics; you can statistically prove anything if you have enough samples and you can steer away from those that do not agree with your hypothesis.

Of course, when you know all this, you can start to recognize faulty thinking and start to actually test the evidence for your dysfunctional beliefs. Our brain is an amazing piece of equipment and we have the power to use it to our advantage; most of us have had great success using this power to hold ourselves back and *succeed at failure*.

Denisia J. Hockley

It wasn't naughty when it was in my head.

Time and time again, people argue *for* hitting children. "My father hit me, and it didn't do me any harm." *Aah*, yeah, *it did!*

We continually hear complaints because "society has gone too far" and "you're not even allowed to hit your kids anymore." Back in the dark ages, the same things were said about beating you wife; it was expected and very socially acceptable to beat the wife to keep her in line. Think about it! Go back further, and it was quite common for a father to loan out his thirteen-year-old daughter to friends for sex; true fact!

So do not put too much weight on things being 'okay' because the last generation did it.

Hitting children doesn't teach them anything about what they did and why it may not have been the right or productive thing to do. It does teach them that when one doesn't know how to handle a situation, it is appropriate to use violence! They also learn that if they make a mistake, have an accident, or simply screw up, they would be crazy to go to their parent for backup because it will result in consequences totally unrelated to the situation. With very rare exception, when parents go looking for help because their child is hitting, biting, or otherwise getting physical with other children, they are children whose parents believe hitting is appropriate discipline. They will minimize it by saying they *only* smack on this or that part of the body; hitting is hitting! Of course, there is the "I had to smack her because she was going to touch the stove!" No, you didn't have to smack her; you needed to pick her up and away from the dangerous situation. If you do not have time to be a parent, please do not have kids!

Here is a novel idea; how about asking a child why they did what they did. I promise you they had a rationale; it may not make sense to you, but there was a reason, and it was not just to be *bad*. And how about getting down at eye level and explaining why certain behavior is not okay and providing them with an alternative behavior to achieve what they want. "But the child is too young for an explanation," you say! No, he isn't. Infants are way smarter than you think, and from the day they are born, you should be talking to them intelligently and using your words, body language, facial expressions, and role playing abilities to communicate. Not rocket science! You were once a child too. You want respect from your child so start by giving it! You want communication, trustworthiness; they will do what you do, not what you say.

Logical consequences means fixing the damage, apologizing where appropriate, learning how and why not to do it again, and knowing how to get help in preventing a repeat offense. Aggression and abuse are not logical consequences for any behaviors or incidents.

Small children usually do not understand the difference between telling lies and stories. It certainly doesn't help when a parent tells her "Do not tell Daddy" or "This is a secret from Mummy." Until now, she thought secrets were for surprises and presents, but it seems they can also be for something Dad did and doesn't want Mum to know because she might get angry or one of those confusing things where he is allowed to do a behavior when he is with Dad but not when he is with Mum, so it can't be the behavior that is wrong! One of the many confusing things grown-ups do that Junior just has to try and work out for himself by trial and error, experimentation, and more scientific experiments to manipulate until he gets results that work for him.

For most people, life is a never-ending struggle for approval, in a perfect world everyone would know how to make sure little people grow up feeling *good enough to be loved*. As psychologists, we will tell you that you do not need the approval of others, that you only need to be loved, understood, and respected by the person in the mirror. That has become a necessary adaptation of the truth, but it does not stop that innate yearning to make up for the emotional losses from childhood. In reality, we all need to feel love and to feel that we are love-worthy!

When discussing this with clients, I ask them, "Who was it in recent history who had the approval of millions, who had unquestionable talent and legendary brilliance but spent their entire life seeking love, identity, and the approval of one man?" For this person, the only time he felt *good enough* was when he was center stage, and was it a coincidence that this was the only time his father communicated approval, love, and value for who he was. As an adult, he did many things to write over his damaged hard drive, and he found that as long as he kept on his one *identity hat*, that of an amazing performer, the identity for which his father demonstrated approval, then he was nearly *good enough*, but sadly, and his amazing life was in fact very sad, he died without ever really feeling good enough to just be little Mikey. I need to emphasize that this is not about blame because his father was once little Joe, also just trying to learn how to make *his* world work (in remembrance of Michael Jackson).

This is probably is good spot to share a letter I wrote on behalf of a courageous ten-year-old young lady whose parents had recently split, and she came to me for counseling so that she could *manage* her parents separation.

Dear Mum and Dad,

I need to write this because since you split up, I know you are both going through some hard times, but I need you to understand what it is like for us kids. Kids don't think the same way as you do; we blame ourselves for everything even if you *do* remember to tell us it is not our fault. We still wonder if something we did or did not do would have made you split up or stay together. We worry that we might have to take sides and that maybe one of you might go away, and we won't get to see you both. Please understand that no matter what either of you did, we still love you both, and we don't want to hear about what Mum or Dad did wrong! Seeing you fight, argue, or cry makes us sad because we don't know how to fix it, and we worry about you both even if you tell us not to. Mum and Dad, please do not do the following:

- Don't try to get us to keep secrets from mum or dad.

- Don't try to get information from us about what Mum or Dad did or said when we were with them.

- Don't tell us your problems. We are kids; we can't be your parents or your therapist. Telling us your problems makes

17

us worry about how we will all survive this. We worry about the future!

- Don't use us to send messages between you both.

- Don't try to compete with each other by giving us presents; we would rather have you give us your attention and make the time we spend together about you and me and not about the marriage problems.

- Don't pick favorites between me and my brothers/sisters we don't understand, and that makes us fight even more.

- Don't let us break the rules and have bad behavior just because you want to be seen as the good parent, which is another way of confusing and using us.

- Don't say mean things or even make bad jokes about Mum or Dad when we are together.

BUT DO:

- DO spend time with me and make it because you want to be with me, not just that you don't want Mum or Dad to be with me; this just makes me feel like no one really wants me.

- DO remember when I am staying with you to spend that time *with* me. Your breakup is not just about the two of you; I am missing you too.

- DO understand that I feel bad that I can't be with both of you at the same time, and I worry that you will be mad if I have fun and still love Mum or Dad. You need to know that even though I am smart, I am still a kid, and this is really hard for me; more than ever, I need you to work together to be my parents even though you have split up and even if you both get new partners.

Another way that we confuse children is with fantasy, secrets, stories, and lies. We use most of these to either entertain, teach, or protect children, and yet when they use the same methods to either protect themselves from unpredictable grown-up responses or to comply with mum or dad whispering that "We need to keep this a secret from Mummy" not only do they get rather confused when they get into trouble, but they also have to deal with parents and teachers discussing the dreadful issue (stigma) of the child's label as a liar!

If you find your child telling a lot of lies, ask yourself whether you have shown them an environment where it is safe to tell the truth when they make a mistake or screw up. Discipline, better termed *behavior education*, needs to parallel logical consequences. Logical consequences of breaking a new toy are that the child no longer has that toy. It isn't logical for Dad to start yelling about the fact that it cost $300; way to confuse a kid. It's okay to break a 50-cent toy but not a 300-dollar one. Do I really need to explain this one further? On the subject of toys, I had a mother who smacked her child because the toy broke while the child "played with it the wrong way."

Rudolf Dreikurs wrote a brilliant book in the eighties called *Happy Children*; it's out of print now, and he has others, including *Children the Challenge*. Personally, I don't think his newer ones are as excellent as *Happy Children*, but he certainly has all the right ideas and explains logical consequences in fine detail. I really like an easy, to the point read, and *Happy Children* was that.

We all need to be seen and heard, especially children!

You need answers! Well so does your child!

Remember, children are not naughty, and they do not go out of their way to do bad behavior. For the most part, they are just little scientists learning how their world works by cause and effect and, like all scientists, how to manipulate variables. "So when I do *this*, Mum screams, and since she isn't going to explain that to me, I will just have to do it again and again until I work out the relationship between the two events." When Junior does something you consider naughty, he had a reason; you may not understand it, and it may make no sense at all in the adult world, but he had one. Instead of going crazy, why don't you get down to eye level and find out what he was aiming to achieve. It may well have been to get your attention, but he is a kid; maybe he *needed* your attention!

Remember too that the rules and boundaries change on a daily basis when you are little. How would you cope if next time you stopped at a red light, a cop booked you saying that this week green was the stop light? You don't think that makes sense? Okay, but remember the kid, who last week wasn't allowed to feed himself, wore diapers and got into trouble for the great picture he drew on the wall with vegemite. Then mum gave him a spoon to feed himself and sat him on a strange seat with a scary big hole in it to do pee.

How much research and scientific breakthroughs would we have in the world if every time scientists got something wrong, we punish them? How much progress would we make if a scientist did not try a number of different things to see what it takes to change outcomes?

Your little scientist has to keep testing the rules and boundaries because in her world things change all the time, and since you don't make time to explain these things, she will just have to keep testing causal relationships. But don't worry. Keep punishing and screaming at her, and she will soon give up trying to learn what makes her world work, and that IS sad.

Be reasonable and respectful to your child. If you are in the middle of watching a TV show and I tell you to do this and do it now, we both know what you will tell me to do! And yet we will say to a child "Go to bed now" with no respect for the fact that they are in the middle of doing something (likely as not you are going to criticize him later in life for never finishing things). The reasonable thing to do is something like saying "In ten minutes" or "When that program finishes, we are going to get ready for bed."

On the subject of finishing things, time and time again, I hear parents complain because Junior never sticks to anything. He tried six different musical instruments and five different sports and did not like any of them. It's called being a kid and testing out life's smorgasbord, enriching his tapestry by experimenting with what life has to offer.

I also keep hearing parents say "She refuses to go to sleep." Is there anyone out there who has never lain in bed trying to get to sleep, telling themselves over and over to go to sleep, doing all sorts of things to force themselves (often unsuccessfully so they reach for pills or alcohol) to sleep, and yet Ms. Two-Year-Old is supposed to have that skill— she is supposed to just go to sleep on demand!

Am I the only one that sees that as totally unreasonable?

Denisia J. Hockley

I mentioned earlier that parenting is the same as managing any other relationship and requires communication, respect, and reasonable language; hitting, screaming, verbal abuse, insults, putdowns, and being told what your faults are is *not okay*! When was the last time you responded favorably to any of these things?

Sure hitting will stop behavior—well, stop it happening in front of you maybe! Junior runs through the house with a glass of red cordial and trips on your white rug, breaking the glass and making a bright-red stain. Is the logical consequence you telling him he is stupid and naughty and to go to his room while you clean up his mess? *Or* could you call it what it is, an accident, and get junior out of the way of the broken glass? he can go get the brush and pan for you by way of contributing to the clean up! Together you can discuss maybe plastic glasses and red cordial for the kitchen only. (If you really must buy the stuff, I'm pretty sure your kids do not do the grocery shopping.)

Oh, and don't get me started on the "My kid will only drink coke and eat chips. It's not my fault my four-year-old is obese. He will only eat junk." Last I knew, a four-year-old neither had a paying job nor did he do the cooking or shopping. Until they go to school, they don't even know half these things exist, so please do not insult all of our intelligence by blaming poor nutrition on the kid. Again, this is not about blame! It is about realizing you are *responsible*, you are the adult, and you have the power to make changes. Blame leaves you powerless to make changes where taking responsibility, owning your mistakes, allows you to make changes and better choices.

When you are 'so-called' disciplining your child ask yourself if you are making the time to educate, guide, and support the child or are you just enforcing your perceived right to *control*. Are you repeating your parents' way of raising you? Are you too much in a hurry or too locked into faulty thinking of your own to put in the effort needed to undo the negative social learning your child has acquired to date. Are you too stubborn to accept that you got it wrong and need to make changes?

Children are conditioned to do behaviors that they perceive will make their world work!

Again! Children are conditioned to do behaviors that they perceive will make their world work! Stay with this concept until you really understand it! They really do try out all sorts of good behaviors before they resort to the less rewarding but functional, "bad" behaviors.

Denisia J. Hockley

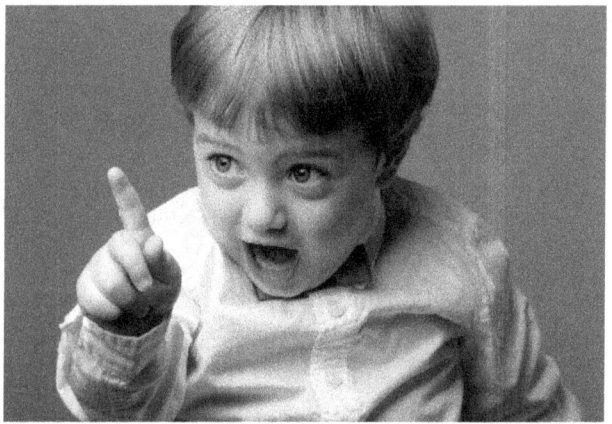

Hmm, wonder where he picked this gesture up?

If your teenager yells all the time, is it possible that their volume has actually increased quite gradually over the last ten years because they do not feel heard? Remember, some of those old clichés, "Children should be seen and not heard," "Do as I say not what I do," "Do it because I said so," "I'm not going to explain myself to a child," "You should respect all adults regardless of their behavior," and "Don't answer back." I'm sure you can remember the ones your parents used on you just as they can remember what their parents said to them. Exactly what is the age one is allowed to have an opinion? Of course, parents have to make many choices for children, but how about letting them make all the ones that are not life threatening. A simple test to apply is: How would you respond in the same situation? Are you being reasonable and respectful in your level of control in any given situation?

At Least If I Don't Try, I Can't Get It Wrong

Learned helplessness: So often Missy makes a good effort at getting herself dressed, making a snack, or helping mummy with the dishes only to be told or shown that her efforts were not good enough and it's better if "Mummy does it for you." So what if she goes out with odd socks and a bad color combo, she is three years old; her sense of self is more important than what people think of her fashion choices. If you have to rewash the dishes, at least don't do it in front of the child. You will be complaining when he is ten and refuses to do the dishes for you.

Denisia J. Hockley

It's so hard having perfect parents; I will never be good enough no matter how hard I try!

Let me remind you that everything I have written in reference to your child also refers to the child in you, the child your parent was (and possibly still is), and the child you are married to. I don't care how independent, big, strong, and bulletproof you are; if you are a mere humanoid, you do need nurturance, we all do! Sadly, many missed out on adequate attention, respect, and nurturing when they were little, but it's never too late, and as nice as it is to have someone to nurture you, sometimes you just have to do it for yourself. Spend some time and effort looking after your wants, needs, and feelings—just as I hope you do your kids.

Grow and Evolve but
Do Not Grow Up
or
Grow Old

As I have emphasized, the only way to get good results from anyone of any age is to focus on their strengths, so any time you start a sentence with "The trouble with you is…" just bite your tongue and think of something better to say! It is probably only your opinion anyway, *and* you really are not the final word on how other people should think and behave. Often an opinion slash insult is prefixed with "I am only telling you for your own good," pointing out what you believe to be someone's (especially a child's) faults is not helpful; try making helpful, positive suggestions as to a better way they might like to approach the situation rather than giving them the privilege of your definitive opinion.

Denisia J. Hockley

Finger wagging is aggressive!

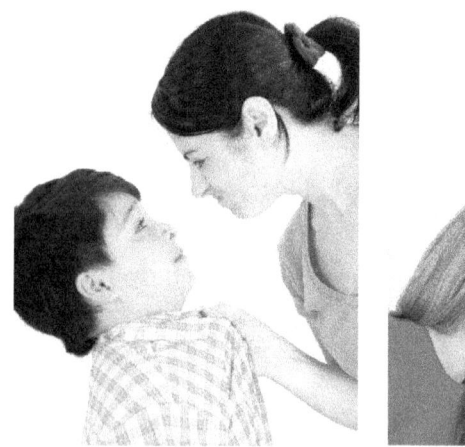

The difference in parenting styles between these two mothers may look minimal to you. If you can't see it ask your child to explain it to you!

Sick Sibling Syndrome (SSS)

So one day, I'm this kid with my own pair of big people who are so crazy about me; they get all excited when I say a new word or draw a picture or do just about anything. Then along comes a baby, and not only do they like him better than me, which is dumb because he just cries and lays there and I can do all sorts of cool stuff now, but they also seem to think I'm all of a sudden grown up and should look after him too. It's not enough that Mum spends all *our* time feeding and playing with it, but they keep giving it my stuff: my baby clothes and toys I still wanted to play with; next thing you know, they will be giving it my room.

In a normal (whatever that means) family, this transition of the "intruder in the house" tends to work itself out, as long as the parents are reasonably bright. However, when new baby has a disability or chronic illness, firstborn has issues that either go unnoticed or get put down to "bad behavior." Often this is confounded by the fact that firstborn, big sister, is extremely loving, caring, and protective of her sick sibling.

We see evidence of SSS in kids, teenagers, and adults, depending on how it has been managed, or even recognized, over the years. The child grows to understand that her parents have to give more time to Junior because of his disability, and she "gets it" that she has to make sacrifices too. She doesn't complain; she loves him and would do anything for him. But inside her is still a normal kid who wanted and needed more attention than she got, and she has confusing mixtures of resentment, abandonment, and neglect confounded by guilt for having these feelings.

As I have said before, you arrive in this world egocentric with rights and needs that your environment may not be able to meet. You need two healthy parents with the time and resources to nurture and attend to you; you may not get this, but you still need/want it! And when your needs are not met, you get frustrated and angry; then later, when you are old enough to understand some of the reasons you missed out (like a mum who was too sick to care for you), you will likely feel guilty for being angry at Mum for never being there when it really was not her fault. Talk about beating yourself up; you can spend years of your life on this one alone.

So back to SSS. Being the healthy kid becomes hard work because you are considered not to need as much attention, time, and stuff in general as your sick sibling. Of course, you are not going to deliberately get sick to compete for attention, but sometimes that just seems to happen anyway. Your parents are so tied up with the baby's needs and so proud of you for all your help and sacrifices, they may tend to give you lots of independence and responsibility. To you, this just seems like neglect, and the only time they really feel a need to focus on you is on those rare occasions when you act out or get sick. You want your needs met too, so you just have to increase those behaviors. Of course, this is not deliberate or conscious planning. It is learning/conditioning because after all, you are still going to do whatever life teaches you will make your world work.

The sad thing in this scenario is that no one really thinks about, or understands, SSS (actually the SSS tag was coined by me). Healthy kid has no clue why she is sometimes mean or resentful to the sibling she loves and is so protective of. Over the years, the healthy kid can learn all sorts of ways to punish herself for never being good enough. She may eventually manifest a sickness of her own, or she may go the other way and develop a martyr complex.

Denisia J. Hockley

Abuse

(A Thorn by Any Other Name)

My readers/clients know that no matter how serious the subject, I will always incorporate a degree of fun and humor; however, when it comes to abuse, I have no sense of humor. I touched on this lightly in the discussion on discipline, but abuse is an epidemic in our society even today when we are supposed to know better. Often clients will start by saying they had wonderful childhoods or simply that there was no abuse because no one sexually molested them or beat them with a stick. There are many kinds of insidious abuse that cause lifelong damage. It is a sad and tragic subject, and it needs to be addressed.

Childhood sexual abuse can be as obvious as rape or as subtle as inappropriate touching by Dad who thinks he is just harmlessly teasing his prepubescent daughter. I once had a lady in her sixties with some major body image issues as well as intimacy problems with her husband. When she was nine years old, she had the start of little boobs developing, and Dad, who to be fair, was not a pedophile; he was just an idiot! When she came out of the bathroom wearing only her panties (which a nine-year-old should be able to do in her own home), he grabbed her little buds and started to tease her. This teasing went on for some time, and her issues developed. Now some of you might say, "Get over it" or "It's no big deal." But it was to her! Of course, I have seen hundreds of people who have been subjected to the full range of sexual abuses and even torture in a number of cases. The point I want to make here is that the type and degree of the molestation does not determine the effect it has on the child (or the adult). In reality, people often recover from a more blatant dramatic abuse easier than they do from emotional and psychological abuse because, like bullying, the victim often starts to think that they themselves are making a big deal over nothing.

The following is somewhat delicate, but victims of certain forms of abuse have found this knowledge very freeing. The human species operates with many basic animal instincts and responses. Emotions as well as physical responses of pain and pleasure are somewhat automatic. Let me use the instance of a male victim here because it takes the point home very well. If a young, developing boy is aroused by images, suggestions, or touch, he is likely going to get an erection whether he wants to or not. It certainly does not mean he invited, asked for, or psychologically enjoyed the experience, but it is very confusing because regardless of what causes him to ejaculate, that process is probably going to feel good. When a situation, which a victim knows is bad, results in a pleasurable physical response the psychological affect can be devastating. They become filled with confusion, shame and guilt. For boys especially, when their abuser is a male, their perception of their sexual identity is threatened; add this to a natural physiological response of confused pleasure, and we have some serious identity, shame, self, and relationship issues.

Females have a similar problem. One of the worst types of sexual abuse is when a beloved family member (often dad) presents the abuse as an act of love, a special secret between him and his "special girl," and in the process, he is very gentle and affectionate to the innocent victim. It may be years before she even knows that what is happening to her is wrong. Later when she knows more about the world and she reassesses the events based on more grownup knowledge, she starts to experience shame, guilt, and disgust. She may have been better off in the long term if the experience was more overtly nasty and abusive; at least the poor little thing could make better sense of that. It can be excruciatingly hard convincing grown-up women that "No, you did not ask for it! No it was not a relationship." You did not encourage or seduce him and under no circumstances are you even one tiny bit to blame! Clearly, this is a huge subject and needs its own book! I just want to highlight a few things that victims often go their whole lives without understanding, and that impact on the developing child when there is no one they trust enough to tell their secrets and subsequently help them sort out their painful and confusing experiences. Why do you think victims of abuse keep it as a dirty little secret until they are in their forties, fifties, and sixties?

We talked about childhood obesity, and that is pretty obvious, but what about the other subliminal as well as overt messages that gradually causes or contributes to eating and substance disorders. From the time you were born, every situation was pretty much dealt with by shoving something in your mouth. You cried and you got a breast, a bottle, or a pacifier. Often as a new baby, you tried to communicate feelings, emotions, and needs and because your parent had no idea what you needed they shoved something in your mouth. As an adult, you use food, drinks, cigarettes, biting nails, and chewing gum, and I'm sure you can think of other things you shove in your mouth for comfort, pleasure, avoidance, pain, etcetera, and even just to be sociable. As a child, do you remember concepts like 'eat everything in sight because there are starving kids overseas" or "clean up your plate, and you will get ice cream." That one teaches you that eating more food than you need is not only a good behavior that gets you approval but also that food is a reward for being good. Don't get me wrong. I love chocolate and ice cream, and I served my time on the weight merry-go-round; thankfully, I finally learned how to balance and enjoy treats instead of depending on them.

Even more serious is when people use food for self-punishment and illusions of control; eating disorders involving starving, overeating, binging, and throwing up. I have worked with hundreds and hundreds of these people, and I have yet to find one who has not endured some type of abuse in childhood. Many will deny this emphatically for a while, but it always turns out to be the case. For these victims, so much of their life was taken out of their control that somewhere along the way they decided (subconsciously most likely) that at least food intake and/or deprivation was something they could exercise control/power over. I have heard many alcoholics criticize someone who is anorexic because they "would never do that". Both the alcoholic and the anorexic have judged "cutters" because they would never self-harm. News flash, self-harming comes in many form, and the more serious ones are usually related to childhood abuse of some type.

A child's internal world, one can speculate, is both lacking in educated, intellectual processing and superior because of its purity and innocence; uncomplicated by learned judgments, prejudices, and censorship. With innocence, however, comes vulnerability. A weed may not look or smell as sweet as a rose, but it certainly is a lot tougher and harder to destroy.

Whether you became a parent by choice or accident, you have entered into a contract to make the person you have created (or otherwise acquired) a priority in your life. You have taken on the responsibility of protecting and nurturing this brand-new person. It was clean, healthy, and unbroken when you got it, so keep it that way! You have a responsibility to be psychic, overcome the insurmountable, be in several places at one time, and leap tall buildings in a single bound! *But* when you cannot achieve this, all you need to do is 'fess up, go eye to eye with Junior, and tell him, "Daddy screwed up," "I got it wrong," "I'm sorry," "It isn't your fault," or "Together, we will fix it."

Learn the most powerful of all lessons…..

THAT YOU ARE HUMAN
ENOUGH TO MAKE
MISTAKES!
REAL ENOUGH TO ADMIT
THEM!
RESPONSIBLE ENOUGH TO
PUT IT RIGHT!
AND RESPECTFUL
ENOUGH TO BE HONEST
WITH YOUR PRECIOUS
LITTLE SCIENTIST!

So you're thinking, "Great! But I'm all grown up. I have already blown it with the kids, so what is the point?" But it is *not* too late; the child in you still wants answers, and the two of you can change the rest of your life and relationships with new insight and perspectives. I have been teaching my client this stuff for many years, and to date, the people I know of that are reading my material are between fourteen and nearly eighty, and the feedback I am getting is really cool.

No…it isn't too late!

As I said before…

Grow and Evolve…

But do not Grow Up or Grow Old

Denisia J. Hockley

Who decided my sox have to match? Stoopid rules & other constraints!

I think it might have been Mark Twain who said "It's a dull and boring person who can only spell a word one way." (If Twain didn't say it, I just did!)

A good friend read my first draft of this book. When asked what he thought of it, his initial response was that there were typos and grammatical errors; sadly, so many people go through life missing the message because they get hung up on the typos! Oh, for the record, in my *Little Book* series, any grammatical "creativity" is probably not a mistake, so be prepared to leave your comfort zone. I love to rattle cages!

As a normal (whatever that means) person, you have some rights you may not have thought about:

The right to be wrong!
The right to make mistakes!
The right to make nonconforming choices!

You are after all a mere human, and we are possibly the oddest species on the planet.

Take a moment to make a short list of the people in your life who impose the "you musts," "you shoulds," "shouldn't," "have to"s, and "couldn't"s (we will come back to that later). Also list those things that leave little or no room for negotiation, things that can or must only be done a certain way. What will the consequences be if you stray from the rules? Of course, you must stop at red lights, and it is a really bad idea to set fire to your hair; those consequences are pretty obvious, but we are looking at the other few thousand rules in your life.

Were you are raised to believe there *is* only one right way of doing something or that if you want it done properly, do it yourself?

43

Denisia J. Hockley

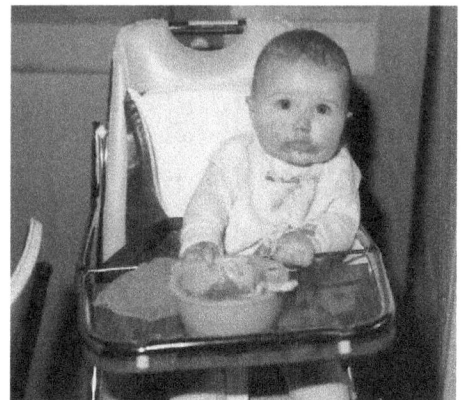

**There are many right ways of doing stuff!
Mine is just the best of them.**

So who is it at the top of your list? Who imposes the majority of your constraints? Yup...*you*! There are usually a number of perfectly reasonable ways of doing things; of course, mine is the best, but yours is probably okay too!

I frequently hear parents complaining that their child "never finishes anything," "started three different sports and quit," or "tried four different musical instruments" OR young people, in their twenties, who are down on themselves because they may have three different college degrees that they started and did not finish, and the big one, "have had twenty jobs" *or* even worse, dated three hundred people before they found " the one."

So what if you get to be fifty and you have thirty incomplete degrees; that just means you are a really interesting person that may know more than most people about thirty different subjects.

How are children/students/people supposed to find out what they really enjoy, are good at, and have a passion for if they feel guilty about tasting the smorgasbord of life. How sad would it be if your child is a brilliant pianist, but you never find out because you made him stick to the guitar; after all, you already "wasted" money on a violin and a drum kit?

We have a trend now for fourteen and fifteen-year-olds at school to be pressured into deciding what they want to do for the rest of their lives. With sensible life choices in terms of physical and mental health (see my *Little Book to be Physically Phabulous*), these kids may well have another century or more on the planet; we need to rethink permanent choices. Seriously, does anyone really want to do the same job for twenty, thirty, forty years or more? While we are at it, and a lot of people will not like this, does that mean spending eighty or ninety years with the one spouse? Damn, he better be good!

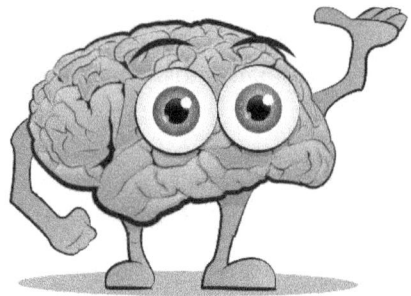

Like most new, eager students, I worked my butt off throughout my university life. I could get good grades, but I really had to work for them. I over-achieved, over-studied, and maybe learned a little more than some others about some stuff, but seriously, I ended up with the same pieces of paper as those people who partied and got through by the skin on their teeth *or* simply enjoyed a balanced life and achieved at an average level.

Ever notice how the word *average* has got a bad rap? Parents love to say their kid is above average, and a C grade or a pass is frowned on. Truth is, average kids are happier, often socially more comfortable, and physically healthier.

Sorry to upset all the geniuses out there, but we are *all* average. Yup, Einstein, you too! You may have an IQ off the charts or a voice that leaves Simon Cowell speechless, but if we had a way to measure and quantify *every* ability, skill, and intellectual process that a human possesses, I'm pretty sure it would all pan out even. Your physics professor may suck at many things outside of academia. *You* may have some amazing talent you have never tapped into because as a child, you used up your quota of things you were allowed to try before you had to pick something and stick to it.

I knew I should have chosen chasing cats!

The kids/people you have compared yourself to, have been envious of, do you really know their stuff? How happy they are? How easy their lives have been? The pretty girl often doesn't have much luck with guys; some stay away because of their own insecurities (she would never go out with a guy like me), while others just assume she has a boyfriend or she is too high maintenance or a whole bunch of other assumptions. The pretty girl often has insecurities because she has only ever been known as pretty; that's her identity, and she desperately wants someone to like her for her. Growing up, she was so used to all the attention being pretty got her that when puberty hit and she turned normal or average, got zits and hips, her self-esteem went out the window.

We already know the dumb scenario where pretty girls pretend to be dumb so that boys will like them. Oh and a big thanks to all the sports superstars that sucked the fun out of playing a sport for fun, like it was, I don't know…a game or something! I personally love tennis, have no clue what the rules are, or how it is supposed to be played. Of course, since I am technically an academic, I could probably learn but I'm really not interested. I just like running up and down whacking the ball! I also love water sports, but I swim like a drowning duck. As long as I can propel myself forward and backward in water and not drown when I come of skis or a jet ski, I'm happy doing my own thing (I think it is called 'fun').

So many kids in school avoid sports because they don't measure up to the best athletes in their class…or worse still they have a parent who yells at them for not winning. And that is a shame! Don't get me wrong. I am totally for education. Knowledge is power; a broad and diverse education gives you power and choices! I am somewhat concerned though about anything that is one dimensional and overly restrictive. Parents, why can't your child choose to be a tradie? Is it so embarrassing to have an offspring who is fit and healthy working outside building stuff? Some of the richest men are builders and craftsmen who start working for themselves early in life, invest in properties, and do not become stressed out workaholics.

Yeah, I said *men*; we are starting to see a few female laborers, but it's not something girls are encouraged to pursue. Before I got all my degrees, when my daughter was tiny, I made a choice. I was not going to go do a nine-to-five job and leave her with strangers. I started off cleaning houses, then mowing grass, then with a big box trailer, two mowers, a weed whacker, and a huge tool box; I became the handy helper and did everything from landscape gardening, pest control, big cleaning jobs for real estate agents, even painted a house, and laid a paving patio. I made my own hours; AJ played where I could see her. At one job, I remember she used her little plastic wheelbarrow and shovel to move pebbles and charged me $3 an hour! Bottom line is I was having a great life, pulling in good money, being the mother I wanted to be, and enjoying a sense of pride and achievement because I did great work with no particular skills or training. I remember one lady did not want me to paint her house; she wanted a man with a painter's ticket. Short story is she ended up getting me to come back and re-do the mess he made of her house. Yes, get educated but in many things…especially life!

It is not popular for a person, male or female, to want to *just* be a mother. Of course you will need to be able to do other things when your kids are grown and independent, but while they are young and developing, being a mom (and of course dad) is one of the most important jobs in the world. The second most important is being a *good* teacher.

If at the end of your journey *all* you can say is that you helped some young people, your kids or student or both, go out into the world happy, healthy, confident, and well-rounded with traits like flexibility, understanding, empathy, compassion, and being genuinely non-judgmental; then *wow*, you can seriously be proud of the contribution you potentially made to not only those people but generations to come.

Let's get back to all those control issues, because that is what we have been talking about. Getting it right! Being perfect! Being obsessively organized! Overachievement! *Being in Control*! One example mothers of new babies will relate to is the Nipple Nazis; their role in life is to make any mother who cannot, or doesn't want to breast feed, feel like she is selfish or inadequate!

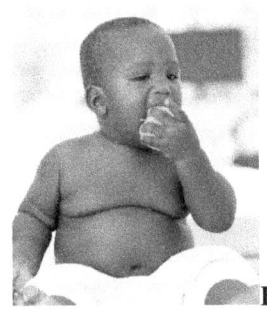

Breast milk tastes good too.

Denisia J. Hockley

And there are many others who know definitively how you should raise your child!

Personally, if you're going to tell me how to raise my kids, I want to see some credentials and a "here's one you prepared earlier." Another consideration when your studying hard and gaining knowledge is to be aware that the person you are learning from may not be right, may be just a theorist, may be outdated, or just never had their stuff questioned.

We value experience, but have you had twenty years' experience or twenty times one year doing the same thing, the same way?

You can come across a lot of single-minded theorists. Psychology has a history of throwing out last season's paradigms and worshipping the latest. At least the old ones had cool names like psychoanalysis, psychodynamics, reality therapy, and rational emotive therapy (RET), but once cognitive behavior therapy got tagged CBT, no one bothered after that.

Now it's CBT, IPT, DBT, ACT and probably PMS, C-BS, and WTF.

Your Child the Little Scientist

Since CBT, pretty much everything new is either just broken down from CBT or is so pedestrian it should be just common sense to any health professional you would want to trust your psychological health and safety with. As I was saying, they throw out the old and replace it with the new, but every one of those original schools of thought had elements of extraordinary value.

It's a bit like advice you need to sort through everything on offer, sift out what works for you (or your client or your child), and take the best from the best. Poor old Freud, as damaged and dysfunctional as he was, he actually made huge, valuable contributions to the world of psychotherapy. Albert Ellis (RET) was criticized for being too full on, too confrontational, which in terms of therapies is a bit like saying do not use that medicine because it is too potent. Well dah! Dilute it! I use a lot of RET, but I take the appropriate dosage, elements, and application relevant to the individual client.

I had a lecturer at university who took us for child psychology; he was an old guy having it off with a seventeen year-old student and had his own kids from five to seventeen years old, who reportedly were pretty screwed up. Just the things he would say in class had me and other students who were also mothers thinking, *This guy has never been near a real, live baby human.*

***Oh yeah, the sox!

Can someone please tell me why wearing different colored socks equates to eccentricity? Sorry, my bra and panties often don't match either.

(If you're wealthy, you get to be called eccentric; if not, then you're probably psychotic.)

Have you ever known, or been, someone who will happily give advice but the recipient is in trouble if they don't take it; often times a person looks like they are being helpful, but it is really another means of control. It is fine to give advice, preferable to wait until invited and essential that you let go of any need for it to be followed.

I once had a client who was very unhappy with her family;

her daughter-in-law was extremely ungrateful. Mrs. X explained that the girl was not much of a cook or a housekeeper and that she would go around and do her housework, cook meals, etcetera, etcetera. You get the picture. This client was actually quite innocent in her intentions. She was genuinely surprised when I explained that the daughter-in-law saw her help as intruding on her territory and pretty much saying that she was a poor housekeeper and not taking good enough care of the woman's son. Truth is she was having problems losing control of her baby boy and unconsciously engaging in a territory/control war with the new woman in his life.

The controlling *gift* is another one; don't want to pick on the mother-in-law, but they tend to do this one a lot, although "generous" boyfriends do it too. It starts with "Let me take you shopping" and ends with "We don't like the dress you want," and you get stuck with something that is so not you, and you're now obliged to wear it every time you see the generous gift giver.

Read this book…so that you can agree with me! There are many subtle ways of trying to control the people around you. Next time your being "helpful," "generous," or "going out of your way" for someone, do a mental check and ask yourself, "Is it unconditional?" and "Do they want it or do I?"

Denisia J. Hockley

Parents are obsessed with controlling children over and above what is necessary for their safety and education. Next time you go to make a decision for Ms. Four-Year-Old, stop and ask yourself what is so bad about doing it her way. How important is it? Think of authority as limited units or tokens—like money, if we print and use an endless supply, it would become worthless (see energy token in my *Little Book to Annihilate Anxiety*). Each day, you have a limited budget on which to spend your authority tokens because you really want value for your investment. Your child begins to realize that when Mum says *no* it is for a good reason. A good reason is *not* "because I said so!"

Let us talk about that first tantrum. I can say my daughter's first was her one and only; she was actually quite old when she threw it, and no, me videotaping it was not playing nice. (I will own that as one of the many boo-boos I made as a parent. I could have handled this one so much better had I known all this stuff back then.) The tantrum went on for a couple of hours; I was lucky because it was at home. It was *so* hard to sit there and ride it out without giving her any attention. Man did she up the ante. But I held fast; she got it out of her system and learned that there was absolutely no gain in tantrum throwing. For every tantrum you focus on or give attention to, there will be ten more to follow, and the more you give inappropriate attention to, the harder it will be to break the cycle, but when you start to hold fast and ignore the tantrum, the child will learn to find another, more appropriate, way to get what she wants.

Yes, it is embarrassing when you are out in public, but what is more important, your child's social education or the opinions of a bunch of strangers in a supermarket? I could list all the excuses you have for "having to" intervene, but truth is, NO, you do not. Worst case scenario is that you may need to quietly, without comment or fuss, pick up the child and remove it to a safer location to finish out its tantrum.

When your little one comes home from pre-school with a bad behavior, let's say she has picked up a swear word, you need to remember this is just like a dozen other words or behaviors she learned this week, and being the little scientist she is, she will gauge the pros and cons of using this word or behavior based on your responses. If you do not respond in any interesting way, she will lose interest and move onto the next new word. Remember, punishment won't make sense, after all it is just a word. Whether she keeps it in her vocabulary or not will depend on how effective it is in getting a useful response. You could tell her that she is going to hear a lot of words like this and explain the reasons why she might choose not to use them in certain places or in front of certain people. For example, if she uses the word in front of a teacher, it could turn out badly for her, but at the end of the day, the choice is hers. Other behaviors they pick up can be dealt with by replace, respond, and reward. With no fuss or attention to the offensive behavior, replace it with another, respond positively to the new behavior, and follow up by rewarding the acceptable behavior with positive attention.

> **Focus on what you want more of!**
> **Ignore what you don't!**
> **(I can't say this often enough!)**

Walk a few steps in your child's life. "I really am confused because I am learning lots of words, and you seem to like it sometimes when I say them but not at other times. I said a word the other day when you had friends over, and it must be a really clever word because you all laughed so much. I like it when I make you laugh, so I am going to use that word a lot because it must make you happy. Okay, I do wish you would make up your mind. Today I said your favorite word, and I got a smack, can't have been the word because it always makes you laugh. I better repeat everything else I was doing then, to try and work out what the smack was for. I seem to spend a lot of time doing things again and again, trying to work out which ones you want me to do and which ones you don't. Maybe it's better if I don't do anything. Might be easier if I just don't do much of anything at all."

A child is born, and its tiny world consists of two big people, preferably one of each gender because that is what works best for them. This is not a hit at gay parents, single parents, or any other arrangement that happens after a child is born. And I definitely am not saying it is okay to stay in a dysfunctional family unit just so that your kids can have a mum and a dad. The fact is however, kids do need both, and while we can't always plan what happens after they are born, we can chose not to purposely bring them into the world behind the eight ball.

So for a newborn to feel safe in this small universe, Junior will need to trust these people in order to later learn to expand their trust to a wider world. Just as he can't go from a womb to a king-sized bed, so he must learn to feel safe with his parents before diving into a crowd of other people. Here is where it gets tricky; junior is neither intellectual nor cognitive, so it is more of an innate or emotional knowingness. Sadly, these early bits of knowledge can be totally false (more on that later). So essentially, I (baby) need to trust and believe that these two big people are perfect, that everything they do is right. Then and only then can I progress to the next level.

If either or both of these parents do bad by the child, whether through inexperience, negligence, or worse, the child has to process the offending behavior without losing faith in the parent. He does this by essentially blaming himself. "If Mum neglects me, it must be because I am not nice to be around or worthy of her time and attention. If Dad is rough with me, it must be because of something I am or I did." Remember here these are not intellectual thoughts or cognitions. These are what I call emotional knowingness, imprints, programs on the hard drive. Pretty much all your issues and insecurities come from stuff that's been on your hard drive since these very early years of childhood.

It breaks my heart when I hear parents actually telling their child that it is their fault Mum has a headache or Dad is angry, or worse still that dad left the family home! The kid already has an innate tendency to blame himself, so please stop reinforcing this!

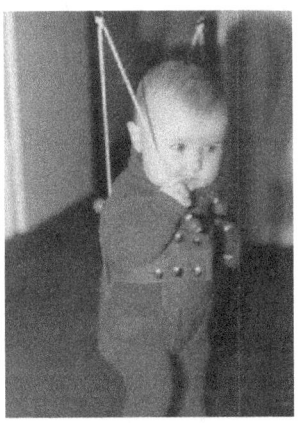

I have no idea what I did, but I won't do it again!

Pretty much all bad behavior starts with a mistake, not a deliberate! Children make poor judgment calls sometimes (just like you do). They have accidents, and they get things wrong (or maybe just wrong from your perspective).

Your little scientist is really just trying to make her world work, and responses/reactions she gets from you and her environment help her decided which behaviors to keep and why. Just like you, she wants a rationale for doing or not doing something.

Denisia J. Hockley

Children Are Born Really Smart and Then We Educate Them to Be as Stupid As We Are!

When a couple divorce, they need to remember they are parents-in-common, not until the child reaches fifteen, eighteen, or thirty but forever!

It's a child not a puppy! Visitation is not a case of your weekend and his! It's the child's access and where both parents are safe and responsible to be around the child should have as much time with each as is possible. If Junior needs Mum on Dad's weekend, then so be it! You are both his parents, and you do not get to divorce your kids.

We all want to be achievers, and we want that for our children; the trick is balance and diversity. A person's *self* cannot be dependent on any one element or phase of life. Kids need to know that it's okay to be average because statistically, we are all average. You may be academically brilliant, socially mediocre, athletically okay, and a total idiot with technology. Of the million things a human does in a life time or in a day, I believe if we had a means to measure and quantify them all, the average score would be, well, average! When my daughter was about four years old, she was fortunate enough to go to a school that praised involvement rather than achievement. In sports events, the kids who came last got recognition for trying. I remember at the school sports when she ran last (which she always did), she turned and said, "Mummy, how come I am always last?" I told her, "Sweetie, see all those people sitting down over there. You beat every one of them because they didn't get up and try."

Achievement is good and can make our lives fruitful, colorful, and multidimensional. But your achievement is not *who* you are (or it should not be). Furthermore, you are more likely to reach goals that are achievable with a level of effort that will increase along with developing self-confidence.

Personal trainers, coaches, teachers, and the like need to understand these things so that they can be in tune with the students' need for positive reinforcement, too often a fragile 'self' subjected to aggressive motivational techniques may just give up once their core belief of inadequacy has been reinforced. We all come equipped with a part of our brain that seeks out confirming evidence for that which we believe (not necessarily on an intellectual plane but back on our hard drive, our original emotional knowing).

Let's talk about honesty. Wow, are parents hypocrites! We lie to children from infancy because we need to protect them, entertain them, or just not burden them with things they are not ready to understand or should not have to deal with. Most of this is fine, but at least realize that the poor kid has to sort out the differences between fantasy, stories, and lies. He also needs to work out when it is safe to tell the truth depending the responses he experiences when trying to be honest. If he had solution-focused parents, he could go to them and confess his mistakes, knowing that he would get support in fixing the damage and working out a better way to handle the situation next time, and when it happens again it is highly likely he will tell you everything.

Or if he feels that he is already *less than*, he will be too ashamed to tell Dad the truth because he doesn't want to get even less approval that he already perceives. (I say perceives because mostly Dad *does* approve but just doesn't know how to show it; after all, his dad didn't.) This can carry on well into adult childhood.

I frequently hear people saying proudly that they are *brutally honest*. The word *brutal* should be a clue! This is often an excuse for being tactless, selfish, thoughtless, and cruel.

There is nothing righteous about throwing *your perception* of the truth around to the pain and detriment of others. Too often what you are calling honesty is merely your own opinion and nothing to do with fact. It may well be *honest* to tell someone they are fat or stupid! What gives you the right to attack a person's self-image in the name of honesty?

Truth needs to be developmentally appropriate; we often need to arrange the truth according to other people's needs, temperament, and sensitivities. How would it be if a policeman knocked on your door; when Junior answers the door and says "Daddy is not home yet," the police officer says, "No, kid, he won't be coming home. He was in a car accident, and his body was splattered all over the road. Oh, and since he probably hasn't told you yet, Santa and the tooth fairy won't be back either." I'm being ridiculous you say! Going too far maybe, but hey, it is the truth, so let him learn to deal with it!

Another news flash. Not only are your opinions not necessarily true, but maybe you need not be so generous with giving them out to people who did not ask you nor had any interest in your version of the truth. Of course, sometimes people do set themselves up for it with questions like "Does my butt look big in these jeans?" "Mummy, am I pretty?" or "Dad, why don't girls like me?" In these situations, if brutal honesty is the best you can do, you haven't understood a word I have written so far.

I had a seriously challenging and closed minded mother (client) adamant that her teenage son was born bad and that not only had she been a "perfect" parent but she had never made any of the mistakes that the rest of us mere human parents have made. This was heartbreaking because the kid is so damaged, and the mother so entrenched in blaming, being defensive and using aggressive bullying tactics, that changes seem highly unlikely in that family dynamic. In fact, Mum is such a bully the son has a type of Stockholm syndrome, in that he is on his mother's side because he "knows" that he is in fact a bad child and everything in the universe really is his fault.

There was a time when every second mother was diagnosing their child as having hyperactivity disorder. That label has changed these days; a few others have taken its place, and mothers/parents continue to diagnose children instead of parenting them. Please note, I am not in any way taking away from children with genuine organic brain disorders or other psychological issues, but these are a lot rarer than one would think when listening to some parents. For many, it is easier to have a sick child than to admit, that like the rest of us, your parenting skills need help, your understanding of infants' intellectual, social, and psychological development is lacking, and that your child needs some changes made in the home environment so that she can learn better, more appropriate, and rewarding behaviors. *And* maybe you as the parent need to swallow your pride and say, "Hey, I got that wrong. I'm not perfect, but I will try to do better!

Denisia J. Hockley

Among some of the stupid things we say to kids are "Grow up," "Stop being immature," and "You're being childish." Well, the growing up is a slow process, which starts at birth and never stops (one would hope), and the kid is probably doing it at about the appropriate rate. I have a huge problem seeing what is wrong with a child being childish; as a matter of fact, I think adults should try it more often; it might help them lighten up. As for maturity, very over-rated and so lacking in so many adults, it really is a bit rude to criticize children for not being mature.

I will say this several times throughout my books: grow and evolve but do not grow up or grow old. People get conditioned by what they hear; growing up, you heard your parents say things like, "When you get to my age...you can't do 'X' anymore *or* memory goes *or* joints don't work!" (Read my *Little book for Your Magical Mind*.) You get brainwashed to believe a bunch of excuses for getting lazy once you hit forty, and sadly you start to become old and decrepit because that's what you believe should happen.

Rubbish!   Use it or lose it.

Age is a state of mind; your physicality is affected by how you care for it, not how long you have had it! I remember when I was twenty-something, I was skiing when I met this skinny, old guy on antique skis; he was doing cross country (the hard stuff). He was eighty-four years old and probably fitter than most of the thirty-year-old men I see in my practice!

Back to some serious parenting issues.

Hitting children *is* abuse!

Degrading, teasing, insults, use of any demeaning words *are* abuse! Neglecting a child in any way is abuse! (Neglect and abandonment can take place without you ever leaving the room.)

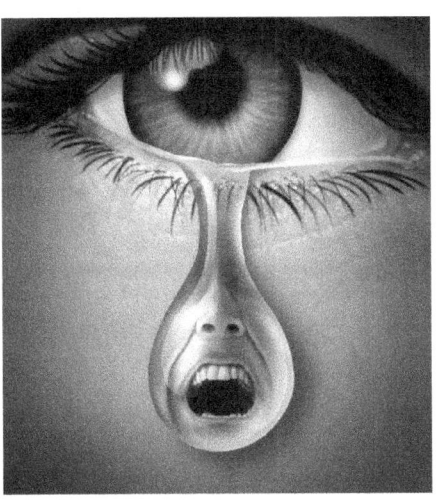

Denisia J. Hockley

Allowing your child to be obese is most definitely abuse. You are the adult; you do control the money and the food so you do not get to say that it is not your fault because Junior "wont" eat healthy food or won't stop drinking Coke.

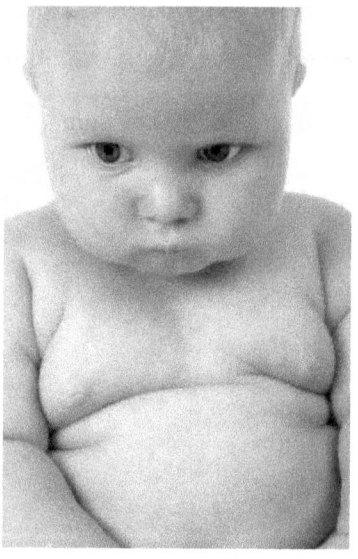

Putting your child in a situation where they have to mediate your relationships, parent you, worry about your finances, and worry about your drug and alcohol problems is abuse!

Television advertising is making a big impact with commercials describing the horrific consequences of smoking and substance abuse; unfortunately, children are seeing these programs and getting anxious because their parents could be killing themselves, and the child can do nothing about it. So many kids and teenagers tell me that they have asked Mum or Dad to stop smoking and/or drinking so much. Is your behavior is telling your child that you do not care about him enough to try and live as long as you can to be there for them?????

Next time you're involved in a conversation about young people and their bad behaviors, you might like to look in the mirror!

Denisia J. Hockley

The Voices in My Head!

We all have a colorful personal world in our heads; there is the dialogue that is always there in one form or another, guiding, processing, nagging, criticizing, and one would hope also, encouraging, supporting and reassuring us. When is a thought a voice? What is it like to be inside the head of someone with true psychosis? Where is the line between nagging thoughts and memories of abusive voices and those audible hallucinations that frequently take over a person's life?

People like to adopt an "us and them" attitude when it comes to "other people" with mental health disorders, especially the more debilitating ones like bipolar and schizophrenia. It makes you feel safer when you can distance yourself from the severely damaged person or victim by convincing yourself that you are totally different by virtue of culture, education, or socioeconomic status, and when that fails, you can always fall back on something like blame. A rape victim is often blamed for his or her circumstances by what they should or should not have done, worn, drank, smoked, whatever! The poor, the unemployed, druggies, alcoholics are not like you! You could never end up on the street or in a psychiatric ward! Keep thinking that if it makes you feel safer, we all need coping strategies.

We often wear rose-colored glasses to help us only see the good around us, and that is okay to a point. Often the people who suffer from depression are too in touch with reality; truth is, life often does suck! Positive thinking is not being able to say "Life is always wonderful," or "My glass is always full of butterflies and rainbows," positive thinking (or being) is "Okay, this sucks. I can have a little tanti, a bit of a cry, hit a punching bag (should be one in every home) to get my emotions out, but after I have my emotional response, because I am a human and that is okay, then I am going to get up, get back in the ring, and do the best I can with what I have! *That* is being positive!

If your friend's life has just fallen apart, telling them there's always someone worse off is seriously not helping! It's just like telling someone with depression to snap out of it.

Back to parenting. Your child is twenty-one and still your baby but is out in the world being a grown-up. He has a life you do not even know about! Firstly, do not be too hard on yourself; this can be hard and confusing. You are still the parent, and of course, you want to protect them, which kinda means you need to know what they are doing, but they may not choose to share all their secrets with you. But what if they are taking drugs, making bad choices, struggling with life issues? What if they are not telling you everything (that is not even a "what if" because they are definitely *not*). How can you control them? Sorry, did you just say you don't want to control them? Yeah, you do! Because it makes you feel more able to protect them from things like making mistakes, especially the ones you made, or to avoid the type of life you do not want for them! I said this was going to be hard because he will always be your baby boy, but he is also a young man, and you already had about fifteen years or more of programming his hard drive.

Your Child the Little Scientist

Take a moment now to review yourself as the little scientist your mother/father raised, and look at the programs on your hard drive! Did you pass some of those on to your kids or maybe the extreme opposites or some alternate form? This is not an exercise for you to beat yourself up but a chance to review, learn, and grow!

Remember, earlier on, I explained that **this is not about blame!**

Blame is a cancer that serves no one. We are a society that always looks first at who we can blame instead of how we can solve the problem! Something goes wrong in a classroom at school, and the first question is always "Who did it?" or "Who is at fault?" Blame's healthy cousin is responsibility! With taking responsibility comes power, power to learn, to grow, and to change! Often we do not take responsibility because life/environment has taught us it is not safe to be honest.

Have you and I screwed up as parents? Yes! Did your parents create a lot of your issues? Yes! Did their parents etcetera, etcetera? But we were all doing the best we knew how based on our own history, beliefs, and stuff on our hard drive. The further back in history you go, the worse the parenting was.

Denisia J. Hockley

So you're an adult, and you have grown kids. Look at your parent not only as the grumpy old bastard that screwed you over but also as the three-year-old little scientist who was just trying to make his world work. (Sadly, his parents had not read my *Little Books*.)

So now look at your kids. Own what you could have done better, but be fair with yourself! Kids, look at Mum, then look at Grandpa. Use what you learn to rewrite your hard drive, especially those programs that tell you that you are not good enough and that you do not have the approval or love you want from Dad but try endlessly to get from everyone that floats in and out of your life.

Stop comparing yourself with others and what you think others are or have. If you must compare, at least look both ways because at the end of the day, we are all better and worse than others in different ways.

It really is the man in the mirror whose acceptance and approval you really need.

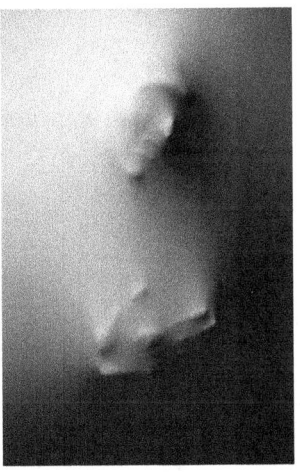

You can hide the things you dislike about yourself from the world but not from yourself. If it happens that you are now a parent of someone in crises, you may have to go back to square one and think of them as a little kid with so little self-esteem that you have to work overtime to prove you will not abandon them.

Denisia J. Hockley

When we have a core belief that people will leave us either physically or emotionally (remember you can abandon someone without leaving the room), we will usually sabotage the relationship to get it over and done with. That is, since you are going to leave me anyway, I might as well have some control and push the envelope. So I am going to sabotage the relationship. If I am your child maybe I will keep upping the ante, all the while hoping that you will prove to me that nothing I can do will ever be bad enough for you to give up on me. Remember, I am not doing this consciously; I am just trying to make my world work and be in control of my pain.

A bit like that first tantrum; how many times you have responded inappropriately will determine how long it takes to extinguish the behavior. How much your child doubts your approval will determine how hard you will have to work to show her you have her back no matter what she does.

Your Child the Little Scientist

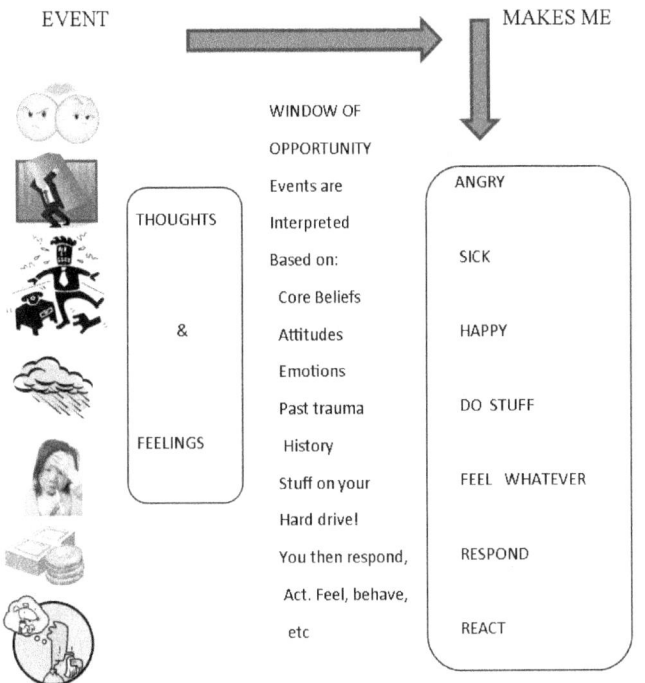

EVENT

MAKES ME

WINDOW OF
OPPORTUNITY

Events are
Interpreted
Based on:

Core Beliefs

Attitudes

Emotions

Past trauma

History

Stuff on your

Hard drive!

You then respond,

Act. Feel, behave,

etc

THOUGHTS

&

FEELINGS

ANGRY

SICK

HAPPY

DO STUFF

FEEL WHATEVER

RESPOND

REACT

Whenever a person says.. "He makes me angry" "The weather makes me blah"

Or any event, situation, memory, behavior etc etc (past or present)" MAKES ME"........

Sorry but that just isn't possible!!!!!!!!!!!!

An EVENT happens OR you remember something: It is then processed through your thoughts and feelings AND based on things like those in the WINDOW OF OPPORTUNITY You respond by getting 'angry' 'sad' 'feeling good' whatever...... GOOD NEWS! This means you have the power to change how you feel, behave and Respond to events in your life!

Again, being a good parent isn't easy! If your kid has an addiction, the addiction may beg you for a fix while the little girl inside is saying, "Mummy, please don't give in to me." Not easy being a parent, is it? Especially if you are one who cares enough to help in undoing some of the faulty stuff on you and your kid's hard drives? The little child in you may be trying so hard to be loved by your own kid *or* so hard not to do what your parents did that you can't bring yourself to say no when it is needed. There is a huge difference between overdosing on control and providing someone you love with safe boundaries to protect them. You will know which it is if you apply the logical consequences test.

If your actions are a logical consequence of what the child is needing and based on fact rather than your own issues, and if you provide these boundaries in a calm, firm, but supportive manner, you are probably getting it right. Your kid isn't stupid; explain what you are doing and why! Then listen to what she says, and answer her with logic and reassurance. Listen because she may make some good points you did not think of which may mean tweaking your behavior to account for this new information.

Above all, create an environment where it is safe for your kid-kid or adult-kid to tell you anything without fear of rejections, shame, or disapproval. Nothing they have done or been through is ever bad enough for you to reject them.

NOTHING YOU HAVE EVER DONE

OR BEEN THROUGH

CAN EVER BE BAD ENOUGH

FOR YOU TO REJECT

YOU!

Denisia J. Hockley

You can discover more books in
"The Little Book" series
www.littlebookseries.us

- *The Little Book to Revive Relationships*

- *The Little Book to Annihilate Anxiety*

- *The Little Book to Push through Pain*

Currently available as E Book; hardcovers available very soon!
ALSO see CD-Therapies available at www.littlebookseries.us.

Coming Soon:
- The Little Book to Address Abandonment
- The Little Book to be Physically Phabulous
- The Little Book for your Magical Mind
- The Little Book to Defeat Depression
- The Little Book to Salvage Self Esteem

Bibliography

Ellis, Albert. *Clinical Applications of Rational-Emotive Therapy*. 1995.

Ellis, Albert. *Handbook of Cognitive Therapy Techniques*. 1995.

MacKay and Fanning. *Self Esteem*. 2002.

Smith, Manual J. *When I Say No I Feel Guilty*. 2000.

Dreikurs, Rudolf. *Happy Children*. 1985.